John Amen

strange
theater

strange theater

strange theater

John Amen

NYY Books™

The New York Quarterly Foundation, Inc.
New York, New York

NYQ Books™ is an imprint of The New York Quarterly Foundation, Inc.

The New York Quarterly Foundation, Inc.
P. O. Box 2015
Old Chelsea Station
New York, NY 10113

www.nyq.org

First Edition
Set in New Baskerville

Layout and Design: Mary Powers
Production Expertise: J. Keith Koger
Cover Art: Strange Theater © 2015 Mary Powers
Stage image © Billyfoto / Dreamstime
Azaleas image © Leslie Banks / Dreamstime
Scorpion image © Tarapong Srichaiyos / Shutterstock
Author Photo: Thia Chempanise

Library of Congress Control Number: 2015930579

ISBN: 978-1-63045-008-3

I was born baffled and have trusted my bafflement
more than my certainties.
—Parker J. Palmer

I know nothing of the role I play.
I only know it's mine, I can't exchange it.
—Wislawa Szymborska, "Life While-You-Wait"

Maybe that's what we look for all our lives, the worst possible grief,
to make us truly ourselves before we die.
—Louis-Ferdinand Céline, *Journey to the End of the Night*

CONTENTS

*

* *

* * *

*

self-portrait @ 1pm

for Sandra

some days it's threading stone
to find the straight line
that runs between waking
& whatever countries might come next

you unfold "what's in front of you"
as if it were a love letter
you're not sure you want to read

whatever it is that passes
continues to pass
Zeno's paradox explains human effort alone

the rest is viral
always eluding
the garrote of measurement

this isn't to say
pollen on yr skin
voice swelling over the machines
you should stop what you're doing

self-portrait twilight on a Thursday

for Frederic Tuten

yr hand slides down the banister
it's 2001 you cough
10 more years pass
the doctor says everything's ok

clocks become decorative
you walk by them as you would any other still life

miniature men in the tributaries
outside the town where you grew up
go on panning the ripples of sin

stumbling towards an altar
no longer there
you grab for pages in the sky

don't worry someone'll say
these reactions are common
the primary colors of this theatrical extravaganza

you smell a storm coming
corral the animals
get the ark primed & ready for sailing

towards open sea you glance back
stone idols perched on distant cliffs
white shirts hanging in the evergreens

you sense that something important happened there on the shore
but new voices are calling
& already the old world is barely familiar

biography

after David Heymann

he stands in the campo
a flock of pigeons squawking at his feet
an Amorite in a poisoned suit he can smell it
strums an out-of-tune guitar

he beholds the Cerberus rounding San Polo
harpies eclipsing the afternoon sun
he tells himself it's no tragedy
that he remains largely unrecognized

he can already hear
the rower slicing through still water
ferry approaching in the haze
the monuments he built
he built for himself
for this reason are destined to crumble

home again on San Marco
he stares at Kokoschka's portrait
how he's worshipped & despised this subject
this face he studies each day in cracked mirrors
in the shimmer of so many pools & fountains

a stooping titan whose features even now
grow unfamiliar in the gloaming
who before his own failing eyes
hath become a stranger

yr opportunity

you let the miniature scorpions
crawl across yr palm on Saturdays they waltz
dragging along their violins

they sting you on the love line
yr cue to revise the tablature
offer standard amends to yr muses
you conduct the scorpions in a concerto
most people can't hear

you say *each scorpion represents*
a sin or virtue you name each accordingly
if you're stung enough times
balance can be restored
the world return to what it was
before you can't remember

congratulations on expanding yr repertoire
watch for strangers eavesdropping in public places
options may expire before you know it
you mustn't miss yr opportunity

self-portrait in the airplane

for Heather

you & the rest of the survivors
were going back to college
taking a sabbatical from yr daily content
the lost & hungry boys
who kept throwing their knives at the infinite

then you're settled in
determined to sell yr swagger
even if you have to remain anonymous
or mail yr enemies a token gift

you've got the proper wardrobe
you're inured to the customary rebuttals
the onslaught of tripe & twaddle
you can handle the reporters
in fact you enjoy a mild to moderate shock

you've done yr homework you're ready
for the detours that shimmer before you

soon you'll be laughing again
you & those crazy ladies on vacation
in some place that has a life of its own

no one'll ever accuse you of hesitating
no one needs to fire the starting gun

you're already gone

make what you can of it

for SJ

it's impossible to "find yr perspective"
this is the way of fishermen
who rarely catch a fish

better to ride
a fairy tale through tireless circuits
the romance of skin & bone

somersault into & out of incidental rooms
phone calls dips & leaps on the tightrope

over & over
find yrself tumbling into a familiar net
flowers in yr left hand
a chunk of coal in yr right

it's yr impulse
to offer the flowers to a mime
you spot on the way home from yr appeal
the chunk of coal to a businessman
who seems less ambitious than you

but no one wants yr gifts
the time for giving things away has passed
now you have to keep what's yrs
make what you can of it

invisible

I know the horror of simple things
a broken wishbone resting on a clean white plate
the red stain on a bathroom wall
images so commonplace
are what haunt me

so I grab my coat from the closet
I visit a man
who lectures about what should happen next
I'm the one shaking his head no in the fluorescent light
a dozen yeses mounding on the table

later I think *had I stood my ground*
a moment longer the nightmare might have shifted

it's not that my volition is buried in a storm cloud
just that despite the fact
I've created quite a clamor
the others raising their drinks in consensus can't see me

I could laugh
who I am so often & now again
arguing with people who can't see me
telling myself *wake up wake up you've got to say the magic word*
there may not be one

self-portrait advent of autumn

for Janet Buck

a week before the agents raid my castle
announcing a moratorium on favorable rulings
I spend hours sketching my alter ego
from descriptions fed to me at a rapid pace
by mentors turned abruptly hostile

the deacons say I've been seduced by pride
recommend that I sit in a cold room & shiver
until the model with immaculate teeth hands me a pink slip

it's my usual defense to curse the gears
the way the engine cracks its knuckles
I swear my strings could snap any day now

but is it worth creating a scene?
inducing a miscarriage in front of the neighbors?

I've abandoned one riddle for another
I'm perfecting my part
until some oversensitive god on a fast track
singles me out for my 13th labor

I can only accept to the extent
that I first resist
so I tell myself *please*
resist

the terror

for Richard

1
always the terror
wound about the strands of things
throttled the soul of the ape

in blackened stars
& stars clutching their relevance
the terror settled

I played toy general
on the last evening of summer
waiting for the dinner gong
things battled outside
things battled inside
my breath coiling & uncoiling

—this the bearded giant's legacy
before his 6 manic days of doing commenced
he paced the edge of the deep
running the void through his fingers

how he was going to withstand being alone
all this sudden & unceasing time

2
I'm told
love created the universe
this too is a ramshackle roadhouse
erected by carpenters with a hangover

there are no perches
when it comes to ontology
we rock in the welter
stumble for footing

though the source could as easily be terror
the uncaused cause bobbing in the pitch
without solace of seed or ash

& of course
every living thing suffers
blasting from the glue of birth
towards that silence we ponder over drinks

our terror didn't emerge from nowhere
didn't rise from small private lakes

it's the untraceable story
in the eyes staring back at you
as you primp or pray
the line in the dirt that runs through each thing
what remains on either side

3
a mad parrot burden
perches my shoulders again

I thread back through shadows
that at some point collapse
into a vortex that has no origin

now & then & later
the heterogeneities congeal
into one indestructible
indivisible moment

you call it god I call it
the terror

4
Richard do you remember
the highway unfurling below the family compound?

I dream it still these decades later
last evening too
had slithered from the gulley
on a sultry night but shivering

ran light-footed beside that highway
to the private road & hid behind an oak
before the search car arrived

a door opened
I couldn't see what in the sprawl
was shoved hard into the high grass
the scene always ends the same

I wish you could tell me
what I never see Richard is it the terror?—
beaten but alive
bleeding in the weeds
then up & stumbling on dented bones
through the groves & fields
its trek of revenge
resumed

one day to arrive
here I say it again
here
broken-faced waving broken hands
teeth bared delivering its subpoena

Richard is it too late to ask for its blessing?

5

I try to recall
of course I can't
how without a word
I became a stranger to myself

convinced I couldn't belong
I strived to resemble
objects that openly informed
concealing a savage intent
there were teeth in the stories
I sold or sold myself

but who's steady enough to judge?—
our trembling also our pride's life-juice

watch me
so pretty so tragic
still grabbing at the infected breast
still groping for a familiar darkness
first & foremost child of the terror

then whatever else

self-portrait on 71st

I'll testify
each fear grows more terrible than the last
each rope extends deeper
each stone takes longer to punch the water's surface

but also a man can kick off his shoes
gain the kingdom in a moment
everything he thinks he is
plucked from him like a single black feather

temptation behind him
will at one with the holy voices

then he's a shimmering vector
piercing the core of each point that would detain him
carrying the future
as if it were a tithe
as if it were the law

for Mary

the son we never had
crawls through our kitchen
linoleum cracking beneath his impatience

he studies us as we sleep
sifting through our trophies & urns
clutching his banister of space

he wanders the dim corridors
glimpsing a bedroom that might've been his
streaking invisible prints on panes & ledges

any moment he could rush the glowing tunnel
crashing a vortex of flesh & fate
the riptide of a beckoning womb

we can't blame him
if he rips our contract from the spindle
choosing poverty or blindness or worse

any quick body to escape his demons
swarming in the quiet
in the waiting

transfiguration

my old friends had changed their names
made various deals to get ahead
but fallen behind
exotic machinery rusting in their front yards

it's not uncommon
for a traveler in this position
to reconfigure the facts according to his earthly despair
I waited at several intersections
for one of my childhood medusas to save me

it was the right decision
to disconnect without fanfare
though I did leave a flurry of messages
cryptic remarks about wanting to meet in a secret place
suggestions about what to bring
how to survive an abduction
by ritualizing nonsense

when I got home
I sat outside writing jokes
worked on my stand-up routine
the air was silent the frogs were gone
that bright orb hovered over the house again
the night everything changed

diaspora

for WB

you leave the party to buy a cake
returning 3 days later with an iguana
asked where you were
you describe the persuasive clouds
how a team of god's horses
dragged you through the badlands
you wandered until you found the slacker king

the appointments & diagnoses resume
men in white mumbling to their clipboards
prescriptions regarding electricity & sleep
friends wonder why you don't lobby for yrself
one of those who's touched the sun
but can't carry his own silence

last time we talked
I saw deadbolts turning in yr eyes
from light years away you demanded
we change our passwords & phone numbers
new information had been engraved
on the inside of yr skull you said
if I would translate it our only defense
might keep the darkness at bay

bird in a bottle

for Eric G.

1
they who are they
am I they too I am

who keep a bird in a bottle
wings plastered
beak pressed against glass

a conversation piece at a company gathering
self-portrait or talking stick

then asking
over folders & gadgets
what's the purpose of a bird in a bottle

2
it takes an act of thunder
to free a bird from a bottle
this isn't something that happens every day

you can't make it mean
what you want it to mean
this is to say
one thing ≠ another

a bird in a bottle
≠ a crusader bleeding on the side of a highway
≠ a widow crying in a vacuum
≠ the jaw of history a moment before the punch lands

a bird in a bottle
is sometimes just a bird in a bottle

3
what came first
the gossipers ask
bottle or bird

smiling at the fillets charring on the grill
champagne bubbling
a red kiss on the cheek

then something sacred will shatter
or a child will scream
or a public building will implode
& we'll flock to the nearest shelter

gather in a circle
holding hands
reciting prayers

around the bird in the bottle

4
it's probably good advice
not to waste these hours
brooding over the implications
the paradoxes & contradictions
re a bird in a bottle

in any case such visions
are delivered in a backfire of faith
transmitted & quickly molted

i.e. we all have to decide
what to cart with us as we travel
what's simply a distraction

whether to find shelter for the night
or continue winging in the darkness
navigating squalls & poachers in camouflage
how best to avoid the guns

5
spring from ghetto to suburb
buds popping on the willow

an hour in the sun on the rocker
with the prowling cats

poppies claim the hillside
a stroll between fields
our guests in the late afternoon

conversations over salad & pasta
re the bird in the bottle

6
only you can say
& even you can't really say
in what way you're = or ≠ a bird in a bottle
whether you're x or y
a reflection of ∞ or an { }
what box to check on the survey
when birds & bottles & surveys are put aside

what you really are

7
a new day will arrive
you'll flutter outside
for air & headlines

you'll consider what you didn't know
prior to what you think you know now

inquiring is there such a thing as a bird minus a bottle
or a bottle minus a bird
noting how the absurdities multiply
much like debt

which is
is it not
what we're talking about anyway

8
at some point
you have to shut out the clamor

the lingering riddle & truncated confession
the bird in the bottle

now shelved & dusty
you could find it if you had to

best not to for a few spins of the moon
a season or 2 beyond the familiar feathers
what you've been waiting for
regardless of birds & bottles

for those who perch on such matters
& those who in their bottles or not
rightfully perceive no need

what we really are

we eat breakfast together
in the scaffolds of light

this
our third lifetime
of mockingbird music

who keep dancing
at the crossroads
by the petting zoo

it's understood
years from now
you'll destroy the house we live in
dirt & knives blaring in the foyer

what we really are
beyond the rafters & plumbing
our throbbing demands o how
we insist on forgetting

hands off

leave things as they are
dead batteries strewn across the floor
a wet glass that gnaws a ring
on the mahogany table

no bargaining with my next inhale
might be my last exhale
stalking me through proteins & a high-octane chaser

it'll be like this
until there's no more
it

others will continue the tradition
an accountant yanking the trigger
the killer's daughter braving cold green depths
resurfacing with a key
that fits some generic lock
in a funhouse across the desert

take all this
the impulse & boredom
with me when I go
wherever it is I go

when the time comes
I'll have a better sense
what's being said
who's calling & why

beyond the houses & desires I can name
one more highway flowing out behind me

castaway

each morning the woman in black
stretched out between the dunes
head propped on her palm
asks me about my dreams

I can't remember
beyond a streaking snapshot
strike the match the curtain flares
then the crest & crash of her interpretation

I spin to glimpse who I was prior to exile
odd diagrams in the sand & seaweed
how I flail in the silence
threats of turning to salt & disappearance at midnight
expiring lifetimes ago

the woman rises to her feet
a breeze lifting her black dress
I choreographed this too years from now
me collapsing into the hunger of the woman in black
bargaining for the pleasure
she sways before me

1969 art project

for Ginny Mackenzie

I tell the madam I own 100 factories
each housing 100 coffins
each coffin containing 1000 love letters
earmarked for the time capsule

she asks if I own a crematorium as well
we have a good laugh over that
she spills formaldehyde on her boots

friends are still
waving goodbye from their convertibles
we'll always be the newlyweds
straddling a motorcycle starving for distance
I've kept the snapshots
a painter in a blue tuxedo
young mothers learning how to pray
the madam in her evening gown
that drags across the graves

we staged a falling star in the background
firing dogwood petals for confetti
as the decade imploded
—so many eulogies then again 1 eulogy
echoing in the driveway

I set myself up all those years ago
just think I wanted to be the gypsy forever

drunk

forget about debate
or erecting a house as common as proof
you outrun light now
yr vision sharper than deathbed sorrow

who needs verses or law?
desire's a magician yanking you
from the hat of yr usual reticence

weep & thunder
hurl marbles & unread manuscripts
reel in the holy answers
from any corner of the sky

of course routine returns
like waking after a near-death experience
but more & more those shimmering threads remain

bridges extend from who you are to who you are
you can use them anytime

our planet's the psych ward of the solar system
then again I can see the moon from my toilet
I mean to say is every obsession part of a darker scheme?
& what's a balanced diet?
granted I watch too many sitcoms
I retreat into my own time machine
perhaps it's possible to be simultaneously grateful

the funniest thing isn't always funny
or at some point ceases being funny
I show my teeth while I laugh
reminds me of being tickled by a molester when I was 8
the door swings open
a stranger in camouflage marches into the room
we freeze as if stumped by a true/false question

the scream of history's heard via two shotguns kept clean
supposedly for recreational purposes
my dry cleaner says there's a love button somewhere
in the clouds or at the top of a golden high-rise
beyond curtains of smoke & sulfur
I don't recognize anyone I don't recognize myself

take 3

the ED at the arts center
offered his right arm to the sun for 7 years

the chanteuse hid in the minks & kept saying
you gotta hit them before they hit you
she raped every line

reporters loitered in the corridor
scratching their clipped wings
I asked one of them
what lesson he'd signed up to learn

when I used the wrong password
the barefoot barmaid
poisoned my drink

& I can't fathom
why I was assigned to the wardrobe department
across that swinging bridge in the old hangar

I found so many masks
I could've staged my own political convention
I stared at my notes until the pages went blank
I forget the details now

I'm waiting for the crowd to return
the higher-ups tell me I'll be waiting a long time
the interns say I'm deceiving myself

I say not this time
not this particular thespian
not this goddamn go-around

summer wedding

for Arlene

heat rises until the bells clang in Baltimore
the maid of honor rents mannequins for the patio shindig
all sorts of bubbly observations ensue

a retired vaudevillian delivers the boutonnieres
we've agreed on a belly dancer in the doorway
the best man invites the witch

once the barbed wire in the bride's jaw slackens
a resident cartoonist begins sketching her profile
the photographer captures Mr. & Mrs. squeezing the juice
a grab-&-grind during their first dance
Father X grimacing in the background

you never know what's being hatched
family secrets exposed during a jazz interlude
all that trauma flocking from yr mouth

suddenly you're someone you didn't plan on becoming

bad novels

for SB

I love mawkishness reminds me of cotton candy
a mysterious serein the perfect backdrop
for an incomplete confession

foils are relaxing in trendy locales
if you saw them you'd swear they were sleeping on the job
& you've got the crapehangers
scheming over any number of dilemmas
forging alliances with gatekeepers & cops

enter the wounded hero in Salvation Army duds
who'll expose the villain & gaslight the media
establish a credible lack of affinity
with matters deemed politically incorrect

the trapdoors in the plot are actually a +
& it's all the same to suspend expectations
let motives & the weather shift on their own terms

here's to arc & arrival
pulleys & cranks grinding behind a curtain
the deus ex machina spinning its wheels in the gutter

a robot poses outside a church
an ape slamming & slamming a human rib cage
against the side of a dumpster

May's a mask of yellow powder
black worms descending from the trees
the ape grunts at the robot programmed to sink its logic
into the jugular of some digital god

they're surrounded by sentinels in camouflage
who broadcast aphorisms
regarding the importance
of paying taxes & tying the knot

ash is already floating in the air
the ape grabs at flakes as if they were sources of protein
the robot collapses to its knees

world as we know it explodes into being
ape & robot facing off
through blinding light & the birth of space itself
each in its own way certain
it's been here before

empty chair

after a photograph by Michael Bryson

what's obvious
is the tenacity of absence
one might infer
I'm smoldering with loss

then again I may've scripted
this outcropping of narrative myself
actually choosing the role of the misunderstood

this could even be the work of a machine
wired by a famous impresario
no longer active in the sky

my possible futures they
converging they arc without flourish they
might as well be weather reports

in terms of a caption
I'm rarely where I think I am

for Rachel Sinitski

yr sleepwalking da destroyed the family Spode
while yr mum clutched her breath in the crawlspace
mud on her pink dress & 4-inch heels

sibs ran amuck on the stairwell
rehearsing card tricks & American rap routines
a babysitter's blood pooled in the garage
yr second cousin left a stain
on yr oldest sister's bridal gown

approaching the plane beneath an August sky
you paused on the steaming tarmac
dark clouds swooning into the earth's green arms
yr family idled behind you at the gate
revving the engines of guilt

like any phenomenon arcing towards its destiny
you refused to look back even once
left those hams pouting in yr shadow
where they've forgotten their lines ever since

business trip

for SK

you arrive the mecca's embroiled in referendum
yr hotel overlooking a frozen lake
you eat locally grown vegetables in a popular diner
where a drag queen reads yr palm
predicting long life & love that transcends the centuries

over espresso you peruse a list of colleagues
scheduled for interrogation during the late show
you improvise a joke regarding posers
tearing yr nametag from yr lapel seconds before
the legal team commandeers the microphone

it's a stellar evening you could say it reeked of legend
the boss left his gavel on the airplane
a clerk from the central branch indulged her fantasy
involving elevators & Victorian garb
everyone agreed yr dance card was a masterpiece

you've proven you can escape yr metaphors
take a sabbatical from yr immaculate whip
now each time you claim
even the smallest opening & move forward
a man who looks like you will be waiting
outside a revolving door in the street beneath a marquee
he too has no idea how all this works

everyman

for John Rybicki

everyman looks like my father
hunched in a shadow conducting rush-hour traffic
at 5:11 when the cops arrive
he puts the gun to his head

pull the loose thread
the planet unravels
yank a nail from a wall
the son tumbles through space

so many fathers I've collected
giants limping across a yard
spinning magic tricks in the half-light
insisting that dreams are stallions you have to ride bareback

their umbilicals protrude
from starched white shirts & blood-stained leather
frayed cords trailing into open space

I float through a bullet hole in the rafters
hoping to kill or at least gather a meal
before the next confluence of father-in-flesh & father-in-sky
that commingling that seduces me
into a tragedy that has no bottom

everyman after everyman
sporting his dull hatchet & broken talking stick
father after father
with the nerve to claim me as his own

* *

One thing's for sure: I've reached the end of my apprenticeship with Dr. Greensveldt, who, to put it simply, is getting scarier by the minute. Do I look like a howler monkey in a tuxedo shaking its fist at the moon? (Actually, you don't have to answer that.) More relevantly, why would I be interested in playing Chinese checkers in a medical landfill? I say to hell with *The Book of Abnormalities* (utter nepotism, irony is *not* its own currency). I'm going out on my own. My own blog, scaffold, cistern, & aqueduct. Give me that diamond-studded scalpel, dr. It's time for a few changes around here. Take 4. Action.

What is it about WTK therapy that leads people to prefer it to more traditionally cathartic approaches; i.e., woodworking or darning or amateur cartography?
Speaking statistically, does lapis lazuli *really* generate a more visceral response from your average citizen than malachite?
Studies suggest that people think of sky as holier than sap?
Crucifixion? Seriously?
(On an administrative note: anyone interested in becoming a board member of the Aberdeen Society?)

Postcard

After 3 years of no contact with my family, I drove to Omaha for the Easter weekend. Crossing the threshold of my childhood home, I was assaulted by the familiar reek of mentholated cigarettes & ammonia, the spectacle of those green sofas & the white Jesus staring from the mantel. I kissed my mother on her anemic cheek, noting her clenched jaw & pursed lips, & proceeded to regress, almost instantaneously, to some version of the preteen I'd been 2 decades before, a 12 year-old on the verge of a volatile breakdown, my father now bellowing from the upstairs bathroom, voice rising over a blast of flatulence followed by the roar-in-the-walls of the gulping toilet, "Hey, is that my goddamn prodigal girl?"

My father the general is dead. What to do with his collection of war-crime memorabilia? How about the unlabeled test tubes stashed in his sock drawer? Not to mention his assortment of annotated bibles? His will's replete with a variety of bizarre contingencies: my sister inherits my mom's jewelry but only if she "drops her vegetarian shtick" & consumes "a variety of animal flesh, in the presence of appointed witnesses, twice weekly for a year." I'm required to "drive a naile [sic] through my right palm with a nail-inge [sic] gun," in order to atone for my "incorrigible agnosticism," should I wish to inherit his collection of priceless Rorschachs. My sister & I are meeting at a Chinese restaurant next week to discuss our counterproposals. She's wondering if a gradual shift towards a pescetarian diet would be sufficient to fulfill my father's testamentary requirements, though I'm certain that my father's attorney will point to the word "variety" in the relevant document, peremptorily adding some quip or another, such as, "Shall we break out the dictionary, my dear?" I'm wondering, in my case, if I could simply lower my right hand onto a spindle a la Rod Steiger in *The Pawnbroker*, though I'm expecting some interpretive pushback given the fact that Sol Nazerman was Jewish. Ah, my father the general. I can only pray (haha! father, are you hearing this?) to any fate or god or demiurge who might be listening: please, may this man's ghost not serve as his spokesman emeritus in the hallways of my mind!

Today while driving to work, traffic at a standstill on the interstate, I saw a Neanderthal—I don't mean this metaphorically or pejoratively, I mean an actual, bona fide Neanderthal—masturbating in the median. The basis of most horror is essentially the abrupt & inexplicable devolution of the familiar into the unfamiliar, & upon beholding this bizarre spectacle, I was indeed clutched by a surge of fear & consternation: the world I knew, or thought I knew, was dissolving; time was compacting, elongating. Induction was suddenly & thoroughly irrelevant; the past had no bearing on the present.

Somehow extricating myself from this paralysis; perhaps it would be more accurate to say: being fortuitously *released*, by whatever combination of internal &/or external forces, I exited the car & crept towards the vehicle in front of me, whispering to the profile of the surprised driver as I cautiously pointed to my left, "Look, a horny, uh, in the median." The driver glanced around, first at the grassy strip between incoming & outgoing traffic, then angrily in my direction. "What? What are you talking about?" he snapped. "Get back in your car." Outraged by his dismissive tone, I turned again towards the median, but wtf, the Neanderthal was gone.

1

you're in bed with yr husband
unfamiliar voices mumbling in the hallway
outside mockingbirds cavil in the holly tree
a man with white hair enters yr room
wakes you waving a gun
firing into the mirror on the ceiling

2

the man in the bed isn't yr husband
you're sure this isn't yr bed
it's quiet as when a spouse mentions divorce
a so-&-so whose tone reminds you of game shows
recites Old Testament passages through the intercom
you start to moisten

3

2 men with clipboards sit across from you
the chorus they're singing makes no sense
& their lies stink like a grease fire
somewhere a leaf-blower rages in the pollen
you hear a muted scream in the next room
but you're the only 1 who flinches

4

yr husband & the white-haired man tell you
you've been trespassing in make-believe gardens
the white-haired man gifts you a strand of poison ivy
as yr husband places a blue pill on yr tongue
the knife swells under yr pillow
god's will's yr will whatever happens next

5

you come to in yr doorway
gun in 1 hand knife in the other
the white-haired man sprawled on a bare mattress
yr husband standing over him muttering curses
you study the mangled blades on the Big Ass fan
odd symbols smeared on the wall with lipstick

6

yr husband's packing his Samsonite
a so-&-so's taped what look like crime photos
to the empty mirror above yr bed
you remove the gun from under yr pillow
pointing it @ yr husband's groin but it's as if
he can't see you & he keeps on packing

7

you wake on a bare mattress & turn to see
yr husband talking to himself beside you
the white-haired man stares
through yr bedroom window
masturbating in the azalea bush
his breath fogging the glass

8

3 black dresses are draped across the bed
yr husband studies each in turn
you grab for the gun on the pillow grab through it
grab for the knife on the pillow grab through it
yr husband pauses to sign papers signing without pause
as if you're not shouting *stop!* in his ear

9
man 1's lying beside you
reeking of garlic & sulfur
a laugh-track's playing through the intercom
man 2 stands over you
breathing heavily behind a surgical mask
you reach for the gun but it's gone

10
you hear a caterwaul it's forever
then grasp you're the source of the sound
writhing on a bare mattress & who's leaking AB+
under the Big Ass fan
no 1 else in the mirror tonight
the white-haired man & yr husband yelling *action!*

11
the mirror on the ceiling crashes
to the red-redder-reddest floor as man 1 prays
man 2 scrawling in a notebook
the rain boxes yr window
you protest but even you can't understand
what you're saying with no voice

12
you offer yr daily lb to yr husband
as the white-haired man points @ yr crotch
tallying numbers on a yellow page
yr husband shoves the drip stand towards you
today sliced from yr right buttock
tomorrow drop a breast on the scale

13
it's after but after what
an invisible line drawn in a void
unstrung to yr husband & the white-haired man
like a snapped guitar string or severed umbilical
yr gun & knife irrelevant & yet this is
what you know what else is there

14
you're sure you can sniff the azaleas
from behind yr window nailed shut
the white-haired man in a pig mask
& yr naked husband dancing under the hose
the world turns green again
the green world & its monsters

15
yr husband recites a nursery rhyme
as the white-haired man flashes crime photos
describing his recurrent dream
I shot the devil with a polyester bullet he says
on cue you hear a crashing in the next room
then the alarm wailing like a mad reptile

16
you wake or this is what waking's like
elbow the so-&-so to yr right
elbow the so-&-so to yr left
their bodies rock & return like anchored boats
the mirror's as empty as a plastic gun
you're @ the door but it won't open

17

you press yr palm against the windowpane
watch the rain scouring the green leaves
clean as never raped to begin with
yr husband lies still beside the holly tree
as the white-haired man behind you reloads his gun
ordering you to turn around

18

the so-&-sos in yr bones confiscate yr marrow
they're not who they say they are
mockingbirds slam & slam into the window
you're floating down a hallway
gun in hand seeking an exit but it's you
still screaming in the room you just left

19

you observe an enemy in the mirror
sly & naked above yr bed
you haven't spoken to her in so long
you point yr gun when you see her
how she smirks back *f u bitch*
daring you to tap the trigger

20

the bedroom door's closed
a clean white towel hangs from the knob
you sniff the AB+ on yr fingertips
a so-&-so's wrapping you in plastic
a 2nd so-&-so emerging from the closet
turns towards you has no face

21

you stare from yr window like a quarantined animal
man 1 naked & sprawled in the grass
sun scaling its way to a full tantrum
steam wafting from the azaleas
you mumble *I wanna die in the summer*
man 2 standing behind you replies *you will*

22

the white-haired man loads his gun
points the barrel to his groin & fires a dry dream
yr husband tosses his dice
tells you to lie down *here are the rules*
don't move even if you feel something sharp
ignore the person screaming in the mirror

23

you wake in a bed that seems familiar
glance under the gray sheet
streaks of AB+ on yr white stockings
the Samsonite hurled to the floor
the Big Ass fan hanging by 2 thin wires
cameras flash in the mirror above you

24

the morning after's the next night
azalea blossoms snarling on the window ledge
you stare through the glass
yr husband stabbing his shovel
into the black earth digging whose grave
as the white-haired man yells *faster!*

25

the white-haired man
squeezes yr right breast with his left hand
his right fingers piercing the confluence of yr thighs
you can't move or speak
between pleasure cinching & the impulse to fly
you're holding a knife to yr own throat

26

through the intercom yr husband tells his 1 joke
about the mockingbird & the prostitute
the white-haired man hulks in yr doorway
waving his gun @ you he says *kneel on the mattress*
yr husband delivers his punchline
laughing & laughing through the intercom

27

the azalea bush thickens like a family secret
chafing since that 1st attack
you recline on the bare mattress staring
into the empty mirror repeating *I don't love you*
yr husband & the white-haired man holler in chorus
wet or not here we come

28

man 1 in the bed doesn't move
man 2 across the room tells you to get up
all the while snapping obscenities
@ the dogs barking in the next yard
you reach under the pillow for the knife
you carry when you sleepwalk

29

you imagine angels marching on the roof
as yr husband wraps his shadow
around you like a toxic shawl
the white-haired man stabs his knife into the wall
sets up his camera in yr doorway
you pose for him as the light comes & goes

30

a hero or was he stoked yr fire
before the so-&-so & the other so-&-so
snuffed you to a low glow & locked yr lips
now the nightly bellows of porn & pills
yr memory flaring its nostrils in the glass
you see his face everywhere

31

what cleaves yr buttocks
a trickle on yr perineum can almost reach
the knife though you're hypnotized
by the baritone of the white-haired man
& yr husband's groan loudening obscene
azalea blossoms wink @ the window

32

you run yr hand between yr legs
bringing whorls of AB+ to the light
finger-painting *god said goo* on the window
@ 5 o'clock you gather yr knife & gun
hide in the closet behind a white dress
waiting for yr husband to return

33

yr husband spends the day on the phone
saying *thank you for the flowers*
the white-haired man tosses his knife
across the room into the molding
again & again after each conversation
until the bulbs burn out

34

the holly's blooming green guns
the grass's menstrual again
a naked so-&-so stands beside the azalea bush
another so-&-so in a tuxedo slips a noose
over the 1st so-&-so's neck
behind yr window you load the gun

35

the house is empty but what house
the mirror too its vision in shards
yr husband's no longer that
& who knows who the white-haired man
ever was with his gun & knife & intercom palaver
you're drifting beyond the details

36

posing on the mattress between man 1 & man 2
you stare @ the mirror on the ceiling
the haft of the knife moistens in yr right hand
it's impossible to tell the men apart
you say to the mirror *I'll bury & bury my blade*
in whoever touches me 1st

37

the azalea blossoms grope yr window
ivy mounts the gutter to rape the eaves
you curse the blank tarot cards reading yr own
wretch-&-writhe into each empty spread
the husband the white-haired man the knife the gun
all point towards death by virtue death by vice

38

the body below you on the bed
the mirror that never stops swallowing
man 1 picks up the gun from the floor
hands it to man 2
who wraps it in a towel & disappears
man 1's t-shirt is inside-out

39

on yr birthday the storm plunges
shucking the holly & the azalea bush
yr husband thins yr hair with his knife
as the white-haired man sketches yr profile
in the red-redder-reddest light you try
to heave yrself out the top of yr skull

40

you wanted what did you want
before the curtains of smoke & AB+
a door to give a ghost a break
a mirror with a wormhole option
knife in yr right hand gun in yr left
you can't cut you can't shoot the voices

The electric xylophone reverberates in the hotel lobby. I'm told the musician, mad from years of drug-induced inspiration, is secluded in one of the rooms, his improvisations broadcast anonymously through the intercom. It's my job to go searching for him, to knock on doors until I find him, until he's standing before me with his unkempt hair & red eyes. "Eureka," he'll say, inviting me in. I'll decline, of course, per regulations, handing him a complimentary Immunity Card (good for one administrative reprieve), before snapping a quick photo & returning to the lobby. I've been through this process I don't know how many times. Now look: 8 unframed & undocumented canvases hanging near the coffee station, no doubt the work of some agoraphobic painter who rarely opens his door, & then only to send down to the drooling world his new batch of perplexities. What colors, what flair, what sense of composition! I can promise this: if we get the funding we need, & my bosses grant me sufficient time, I'll unearth them all—these musicians, these painters, these tormented provocateurs, how they hide in their shrinking chambers, hoarding the secrets of the universe!

XY hurtles from his swing & tumbles to the earth, his head bouncing on the red clay. He lies at the feet of the great mother, the world encased in white light, stars, a slightly distorted ringing. He beholds a future version of himself, knife in hand, cutting a young woman's throat, her blood gushing over his hands. He witnesses a series of grisly images, the final involving his own death by suicide. Then his head & the skies clear; he clambers to his feet, for years afterwards plagued by migraines & odd periods of amnesia followed by synesthetic reveries.

One Tuesday, when he's in his 20s, he remembers his experience of falling from the swing; a door opens & ushers him into his premeditated future. Violent desires assert themselves; gruesome choreographies occupy his mind; sinister strategies drain his resources. He kills his first victim by knife, his second by rope, etc., each act in accordance with the vision that enveloped him for mere seconds when he was a younger XY sprawled on the red clay. The acts bring him a modicum of pleasure, minor arousal, fleeting erotic frissons, but it's more as if he's dutifully enacting a role required of him, obeying a cosmic script or dictate.

He continues with his lurid purpose until he performs (he no longer thinks of it as choosing) his 12th labor (he *never* considered what he's doing to constitute murder). He recalls his earlier vision, how he watched himself, at the conclusion of that searing tableau, ushering his own plunge into oblivion. Adhering to details he can still vividly conjure, he makes his way to a rooftop garden accessible to the public. There, without the slightest hesitation or twinge of disillusionment, he approaches the balcony, vaulting over it to the thin ledge, then releasing himself, face-first, to the concrete below. He doesn't leave a note; he's never connected to the murders, though they abruptly cease after his death; & the fate of earth, galaxy, universe, continues to unfold, XY having embodied his role, however minor, in furthering the plot of life itself.

Or perhaps this is all nonsense. What illusions we feed ourselves, what metaphors we concoct, to justify our own predilections; how we gesture & gyrate, branding our names on the forehead of the sky. But therein lies our reprieve: tireless machines tick & whirl in our skulls, pots & pans boil over in our chests; o doomed creature of the red clay, embrace this fortuity—invent a mission, a script, a narrative; come up with a delusion worth believing!

I linger in the bathroom, examining toothbrushes, 3 hairs on a bar of soap, reexamining the toothbrushes. Finally I drift into the adjacent bedroom & see a young girl, vaguely familiar, sitting up in her bed, her mother poised next to her. "Darling, let the doctor take a look," she says. For a moment, I have the alarming impression that the girl can see me; then I realize she's simply staring blankly, though precisely in my direction. The doctor proceeds with his exam. Stethoscope, various manual prods & pokes; he lifts her eyelids, tells her to cough. I move towards the bed & extend my fingers towards the girl's face until they're almost grazing her hollow cheeks. "Ok, dear, the doctor & I are going to talk," the mother says, "we'll be back in a minute." The mother & doctor leave, & I hear them mumbling outside the closed door, though I can't make out what they're saying. "Hello," I mouth, moving from one side of the bed to the other. "How...are...you?" Outside the mumbling continues. The girl reclines & closes her eyes. I drift back to the bathroom & squat on the edge of the tub. I'll just stay here for a while, I decide, studying the wallpaper, a yellow stain at the bottom of the toilet. The mother & doctor reenter the bedroom. That's when it occurs to me that this routine has repeated a number of times. Now I'm wondering how long I've been here.

That birthday, I swallowed Valiums with vodka, drove dark back-roads, both headlights broken. I made it to the driveway, crashing into an oak, passing out behind the airbag. Jul called an ambulance, & I came to in intensive care, sunlight flooding through barred windows, tubes flowing like power lines. I'd been here before, each survival bolstering some myth of invincibility, but this time I knew I was treading a bloody shark pool, the inglorious end converging like teeth. I told the doctor I intended to get clean. He shrugged when I declined his offer to check me into a treatment center, railed that the odds were mounded against me. Death sat on the edge of the gurney, smiling like a mentor.

1942

Once in a while, the ovens cease working. Future generations stand in the street blowing trumpets and throwing graffiti. Schools are closed for the day. Even the Jewish programmer, perched in his tower, alone night after night, takes the evening off, his lines of code dispersing like chemtrails.

the real problem is doubt

Whatever you do my dear is fine.
It's just the forethoughts and afterthoughts
that cloud your vision.
—Richard Sassoon

resistance is a strange pantomime
the will pushing a wheelbarrow
full of rocks up a hill before twilight
I don't know where my mind goes

I love a story as much as the next guy
but some of these boulevards
dead-end in unfriendly places
I can't predict much
though I can say with confidence
plotlines are freezing
characters are thawing
I still hope to stumble upon a guarantee
somewhere above the cloud line

I keep saying *everything is fuel*
when I should be processing spreadsheets
my calculator blazing like Halley's comet
well I say *should*
I don't know what that means
maybe it's as simple as
the last few hours got the best of me

bardo

I wait by the window
for the producer to arrive

for the bass section
the mannequin strings
the soprano with the purple hair

other wannabes with secret talents
drag along their expectations
as I drag along mine

an intern points to her press badge
blood on her white lapel
I ask if she's the producer I know she isn't
though I've smelled her ambition before
at some other dock or tollbooth
a killer posing as a confidante

the session guys
nod into their saxophone dreams

I smoke in the lounge
I edit my masterpiece
by morning I let it go

purgatory

for RBC

after the Iscariot boys leave
we're alone again in the dining hall
yr arms now thorny branches
Villafrancas bursting from yr overhang

I pluck a ripe sample
from the tip of yr middle finger
sinking my teeth through rind into a glistening pulp

laughter sputters from yr knotted mouth
the waiter says *welcome home my exiled beauty*
boiling water cupped in his palms

you adjust the folds in yr gown
studying the menu as would any debutante in transit
grainy eyes rolling you announce
I know what I want
I reply *I don't*

self-portrait on lunch break

Is it possible to grasp
a life's beauty while living it?
—Mary Powers

surrounded by ballerinas
I'm not sure how my background in math will serve me
still I visualize a world of right angles
reciting theorems with a full mouth
how many times has π saved my life?

then I'm alone again
this has happened before
I'm always lamenting
the appearance & disappearance of the ballerinas

I've distracted myself from the trial at hand
inhaling postulates & sugar
a headache to recall the names
of so many ballerinas I've pursued over decades
names merge into 1 name
proofs merge into 1 proof

I could bargain a little longer
but the route I'm traveling
will soon carry me across an ancient border
this is what I've been dreading

dread on
paper blossoms hang from petrified trees
even my memory that incorrigible hoarder
is inching towards the exit
the critical moment couldn't be more palpable
had I designed it myself I did

freeze in the doorway my femme fatale
I'm telling you our act's the greatest thing since the hologram
let's knock this out & get back to our planets happy

what The Fates decide
has nothing to do with how things turn out
that's a different ship
on a different course
you'll be glad for the way things were written

footsteps on the landing
our breath is their breath is our breath
the money smells like used towels in a docking station
clutch our guns this time
we might need to use them

initiate

for MS & BB

I stir in the middle of the switch
tables floating above the bed
chairs sliding from wall to wall

I stumble to the bathroom
my face permutating in the mirror
outside the cityscape reconfigures
stars are extinguished & relit

in the morning
I run my hands over my wife's back
feeling for the control panel

I tell a friend
the story of what I saw
searching the eyes of strangers
for passengers in hiding

I know there've been others
who glimpsed the rearrangements
the hidden machinery in motion
still I could go mad trying to find a believer

it's grace I'll forget what I saw
in time dismiss it as a dream
the blank night splattered with my fears

some rogue vision that by chance
broke the atmosphere of my waking mind

1
you announce over the drawl of an engine
this is the 21st century
our dreams race along superhighways
you urge me to state my intentions
before the lighting shifts
& such matters become moot

I point at the dead dragons mounded in the landfill
offer my usual tirade regarding
how the great myths have been forgotten
I avoid any mention of swords

you're right that whatever I've said
didn't include a reliable ladder or sturdy rope
by which we could descend into the core of our concerns
perhaps strike water or find fire
another circle beneath the catacomb
where we could pause & petition our gods

2
I pace dim hallways
to forge a prayer
my body can believe in

when fires flare on the outskirts of the city
or some dragon shows its teeth
at the entrance to the next circle
I often come to clutching a sword
I don't recall pulling from the stone

my memory a password fading in the mist
the last breath of a dragon

dying in a culvert
beneath a nuclear sky

3
the scene's the same as before
though the tone's different
the apocalypse has become a slow-motion sequence
has become a vaudevillian travelogue
has become a stroll
to the end of the driveway
to gather mail or take out trash

dragons are piled at the curb
occasionally one revives
snorts & kicks over a garbage can
a sword might appear in a flowerbed
protruding from a pool deck
in a gated backyard

sometimes I find an entrance to a new circle
sometimes in the oddest place
a grocery store aisle
or the path from bed to bathroom
in the middle of the night

4
we've returned from our travels
with a lexicon that gets us where it gets us
but let's not fool ourselves
these circles have been mapped & documented
by critics & rock stars alike
to the point of implosion

we needn't lament how we flourish in the suburbs
cherishing our new mandates
how most of us keep a pet dragon

dozing at the foot of the bed
who occasionally disappears in the darkness

at dawn we go looking
though we've learned how to wait
we know that hungry dragons
can find their own way home

on reincarnation

for O H

after the guitar player died
his addiction a slow progression of minor chords
acquaintances believed
whatever they needed to believe

then the anniversary
guests bobbing & preening to my irregular beats
I mean you want folks to know how you feel
but the bills are nagging
the car needs to be fed
before you've even landed yr next hook
yr kids are building their own houses
singing their own songs

I told a stranger *the sky's out of key*
not that I listen that way 24/7
after all the ear hears what it's told to hear

I took up residence in a doorway
a curmudgeon clutching a tuning fork
others came & went & returned
someone said *friendship's forever maybe*
these days of summer these riffs aren't

you know what I'm getting at
riding my coda of boredom & sex
I keep saying *I don't want another go-around*
but I do
god I do

porch life

for EVC

I've reserved a revolving door
so expect a case of yr favorite toxin
& don't count me out
despite my cloak-&-dagger tweets

I'll make do with a few pages
from Adele's diary I found behind the toilet
but damn this is darkness
a good reminder
I'm in a crazy romance with lamentation

to answer yr question
I'm stranded in a warehouse outside a factory
near a city with no name
& the machines ain't crumbling anytime soon

I need friends I'm not faking it
waving from my side of the street
to anyone who passes yea I know
all my karma's swirling around me

self-portrait @ noon

I stand in the driveway
of the research lab where I was raised
waving a rifle at the neighbors

I can't afford
to discard this story

I slipped on the staircase
now water won't boil for me
each hour brings a new
declaration of war

contrary to classic depictions
the ferryman is an extrovert

are you suggesting
envy's a door
behind which is an empty office
where no one ever died
from not belonging?

the birds nesting in my throat
died overnight

what you renounce
will give you another chance
later

why visit a country
that's simply a passage
back to where I came from?

what you say in one room
echoes in another
these are the things we live with

there's no getting around autobiography
murder by anecdote

the kids in the kitchen
can tell I've been doing
black cartwheels in the basement

hours with books & movies & bills
& what doesn't get said

these days I resist more
& surrender quicker

I thought I was on a ship
singing with the stars
I was actually
lying fetal on a yellow mattress
outside a stranger's bedroom

a time comes
the to-dos no longer legible
appointments are abandoned

people fall in love with surrogates
every day

you keep saying shame is obsolete
you should read the fine print more carefully

it's never been hard for me
to think of guns & flowers
in the same breath

you can't push the mother out
you can't drag the father in

no tracks lead
to what hangs over us

retirement home

for HK

we pack & unpack boxes
staving off the teeth in the silence
our shelves lined with family photos & bric-a-brac
every day a meeting you better not miss

who we are when we're alone I say
should be the subject of our mockumentary
the dance teacher pantomiming with broken glass
the palsied surgeon flogging his memoir

I'm told this is the best deal in town
so why is the taxman's injunction still hanging
like a price tag from the third eye of our mannequin Christ?
standard MO for the intercessor?
all because we panned his original thesis?

shrinking giants inventory their bruises
other curmudgeons analyze in detail
how they've been tricked by dirt & sky

you have to admit it's odd the way we wring our music
makes me wonder if the scream in the night's a test
—our boundaries are made of fever

guilt by necessity

1
yr father raised you his honing steel
each night whetting a prayer
a dull sermon between yr thighs
as you pretended to sleep
in the pink room with the altar

second Sunday in June
I set his church on fire
the crucifix curled & cracked like a salted slug
turning on itself like a teenage cutter
black smoke shrouding the evergreens

when yr father stumbled out in flames
collapsing beside the dry well
I pissed & pissed until the blaze went out
50 congregants on their knees
screaming in the white gravel

2
we raced the janitor's van along back roads
yr water splashing to the floorboard

an hour into Oklahoma
in a trickle behind a strip mall
where a stray mutt stood growling
you baptized an empty bag of blood & bones
swaddled it in the pages of a tabloid

after the oil fields of Texas
in that windowless room dizzy with hunger
you put the red package on ice
as if it were a tenderloin

3

the van bounced through potholes
as you mangled nursery rhymes
a wad of 20s clenched in yr teeth

the line of cops parted like a marching band
bullets & wheels spinning in a ditch
you slumped over the dashboard
2 holes in yr neck still clutching that slab of meat
now wrapped in a bedspread
from the Wandering Rose motel

by the time the uniforms
dragged me through the cacti
you & the tenderloin were climbing
a swinging ladder into the darkness

4

I sit in the devil chair
while robots blaspheme our gospel
my lips glued shut
hands wired to the table

you visit my daydreams
dangling from the courtroom rafters by an umbilical noose
spook babbling in yr womb

when the clone with the hammer mouths his part
the clock in my veins stops ticking
I watch most of me drift
into a '61 T-Bird with a bottomless tank
car & rider dissolving in the distance

what remains—
who's in charge—
watch it call their bluff

folk singer

of course you're suffering
that goes without saying
alone in yr own private tundra
staggering through the snow

the face of some Beatrice behind & before you
head & heart those masters of spin
weave from the unknown a threadbare headline
silence that gray country
where you arrive & arrive already judged

you crave anything that steams
be it liquid or flesh
as long as words & notes keep rolling
as long as there's a chance
of surviving until spring
seeing that Beatrice again

she'll slide a plate across the table
drop her dress to the floor
you won't have to explain where you've been
or dance around yr conscience
o you holiest of fools

trough

for DF

I'd like nothing more
than to sink into a warm amnesia
but this isn't on the docket for me

prime mover adrift in a cul-de-sac
hand reaching towards a doorknob
this is putting it obliquely

push one foot forward into the hallway
knock a few portraits to the floor
leave muddy prints on the carpet

there's no traction when I'm like this
full of chains & politesse
even the ape my father
couldn't blow open the books

untitled #4

after Boston

oh god is all that can be said at times
while a chicken farm rumbles
where a strip mall was before a forest was before that
I get tired of explaining—let my reticence be a prayer
though I might ask later
outside a costume shop or car dealership
what're you going to do about it?
I'm not sure who I'm talking to
maybe myself

I'm debating issues I can't impact
clicking on the same link 5 times in a minute
nothing's changed but that's a small fly in a large room
the rush of possibility's my drug of choice
like the gambler who if honest
isn't compelled by the hope of winning
but by the adrenaline of not knowing
right before the cards are revealed

later I'll be attending a rally
replete with the usual abundance
many are gorging how they won their bets
bragging hunger at a finish line that reeks of favorable odds
in other places where the buffet's closed
a black hole sucks the bones & bank accounts
of every johnmarcos&maria
I know it's tempting to resign but don't

self-portrait in spring

for Casey

at some point you realize
the scaffolding's gone
the wheel has kept turning

cardinals nest in the trees
hills are flushed with new color
you didn't think it was possible
to sing again

all around little explosions are happening
inside you too wild melodies stir
blossoms pop from yr fingertips
green shoots rising from yesterday's wreckage

everything you carted
everything you left for others to study or destroy
you whisper *yes I'm still here yes*
this is what I've chosen
this is what was chosen for me

as if you swear a steady hand guides you
taught not to be certain
this time you are

that door

amidst a thousand bellowing options
I sign the contract
today I'll walk through that door

typically when making such a commitment
I know in advance what sort of scenario awaits me

in fact I've spent hours in many rooms
accessed through many other doors
negotiating with court jesters
swapping strategies with professional eavesdroppers
3 days a week brokering deals
with gatekeepers & midwives of commerce

all to ensure
that what's behind that door
will be well choreographed
I won't waste my resources lamenting *I don't belong here*

but at some point when I open that door
instead of encountering the usual office scene or hotel bar
I find myself at the entrance to a vintage theater
colleagues & acquaintances reclined in tattered chairs
taking in a black & white movie

at first I resist the invitation
accustomed to protocols rote introductions at least
a few jokes deflating the silence

I see the seat with my name on it
not the name by which I used to cast myself in sitcoms
the name I imagine

appearing on embossed stationery & seminal manifestos
but another name
that makes me seem a bit more like a hero

I start watching the film
soundtrack rasping through torn speakers
grainy images jerking across the screen
then I'm laughing at myself
my odd posture & competitive gaze
louder perhaps than I've laughed before

I smile at the woman in the seat next to me
her cheekbones familiar though I can't quite conjure the room
where a certain shudder first occurred so I whisper
just like old times & she winks at me

I rearrange my limbs
the credits begin to unfold
the closing song crooned by a famous daredevil
against the backdrop of an imploding high-rise

I could get used to this I quip in a voice I've never tried
she grabs my forearm & studies my palm
but already the hook is digging into my palate
already I'm reeling myself through another set of doors
into yet another room I'm busy straightening chairs
arranging laptops & patented prototypes
shuffling notes for an afternoon coup

my departure is seamless
her face fading like a logo lost in a corporate merger
it was lifetimes ago I felt the tip of her finger
tracing the heel of my hand
waves of her breath fogging my company wristwatch

I've no idea what happened before what'll happen next
so much collateral sprawled before me
the numbers cowled in black offering their peculiar benediction

I watch my rival for a moment looks like me
cringe as I slip the blade between his ribs
I'm back in love I've always been in love
with who I think I am

retail

fuck the mall
give me the sky
—MP

something's building here
I tell you it may not explode
it may not come forth

but these are hands that deliver cities
they're divining rods

men with forklifts
daydream beyond their usual cranes & crates
& later some new hook will sound

the girls in the window
turn to crones
turn to numbers
in a single season

it's impossible to explain
so much cargo strapped to my wings

what we're given
the streaks across the sky
& what we're given

on restlessness

for Ben

the dark woods are calling
on the longest day of the year
& o the appeal of sinking in boreal depths
were even my lungs to writhe & seize
how the end might be painless
then a blank tombstone
forever windows you can't see into
or out of

I'm never sure what to invest in
unconvinced resolve's the master key
I go back & forth
between clouds & my checkbook
until all tenses fade
no deadbolt slamming a threshold
no loss or profit
beyond the dictates of gravity

my tattered map belies
I'm so often the changeling yet unchanged
dragging the same plow
back & forth the same forsaken plateau
face covered in mud
father's belt chewing into my back
mother sobbing in the bathroom

in my trances I hear the shotgun
the body collapsing in the cornfield
dogs snarl behind a chain-link fence
under my skin an ancient engine's revving
the stills pulse on the hillside

a man with a shovel's guzzling the hard stuff
it doesn't take much

through marriages & jobs
so many addresses that skein of shuffled zip codes
choruses collapsing into choruses
collapsing into one endless unvarying note
it returns: a gypsy wrapped in red scarves & black skirt
dice bouncing across a table
the hunger that swells with feeding
again I show the world
how to starve on a full stomach

epilogue

we built a theater devoid of doors
my parents moved in after the consecration
renting an unfinished room near the steeple

they spend their days watching tv & fighting
drafting manifestos their fans'll never see
occasionally glimpsing the lights below
rain dripping from a cardboard sky

they're deaf to the racket of mortal affairs
have no interest in summer's drunken ways
the sobriety of autumn
snow piling like so many unanswered petitions
& again the rasping thaw

I'm just like my father
another ghost vying for the limelight
just like my mother keeping score in the darkness
such grandiosity born of despair
daddy Z & my mum the yammering Hera
holed up in their loft
decrying the conundrums of the world
while I hide here—

look as much as you like
you won't find me

curtain speech

for Michael S.

after the final show
we attend the final party
encouraging ourselves to stay in role
consider
nothing's a failure
unless everything is
oblivion's always advancing & always plants its flag
we do what we can
to hold the line for a while

frustrations spark in the wings
flaring towards the open mic
as we raise our drinks
lamenting the end of the theater
soliloquizing how the advisory board
could've eluded this checkmate
kept the lights on
the doors open

fact is every dream ever conceived
was at its best
prior to being scripted
before its author was even born
before the big bang
banged
making all these dramas possible

a week later
we're back to our usual improvisations
the hungry gas tank

illnesses that stalk us
the math that keeps us up at night
love we hold at bay & to which we finally surrender
we straggle into our familiar & unfamiliar lives
how comedy keeps becoming tragedy
keeps becoming comedy...
& there's just no telling
how this one's going to end

ACKNOWLEDGMENTS

Asimov's Science Fiction: "transfiguration"
Coldnoon: Travel Poetics: "business trip," "castaway," "1969 art project," "the new world," "self-portrait @ noon"
Cyclamens and Swords: "drunk"
DMQ Review: "self-portrait @ 1pm," "the real problem is doubt"
Doctor T.J. Eckleburg Review: "everyman"
First Literary Review: "Notice," "1942"
Iconoclast: "make what you can of it"
International Poetry Review: "invisible"
Iodine: "what we really are," "self-portrait in spring," "self-portrait on 71st"
Lily: "twilight on a Thursday"
The Literary Bohemian: "hands off"
Mad Hatters' Review: "self-portrait advent of autumn," "trough," "retail"
Main Street Rag: "summer wedding," "on reincarnation," "the son we never had," "epilogue"
Maintenant: "take 3"
Offcourse: "self-portrait in the airplane," "bad novels"
Paterson Literary Review: "self-portrait on lunch break"
Poetrybay: "purgatory"
Posit: "diaspora," "retirement home"
Presa: "biography," "yr opportunity," "bird in a bottle," "the terror"
Redheaded Stepchild: "that door"
Star*Line: "a modern romance," "Preface to an Investigation"
Wild Goose Review: "folksinger," "curtain speech"

"initiate" appeared in *Kakalak 2014* (Main Street Rag Publishing Company; Eds. Richard Allen Taylor, Lisa Zerkle, and Beth Ann Cagle)

"23" appeared in *Writers on the Edge* (Modern History Press; Eds. Diana M. Raab and James Brown) and *Words without Walls: Creative Writing in Alternative Spaces* (Trinity University Press; Eds. Sheryl St. Germain and Sarah Shotland) "untitled #4" appeared in *What Matters* (Jacar Press; Eds. Debra Kaufman, Richard Krawiec, and Stephanie Levin)

"untitled #7 appeared in *I Let Go of the Stars in My Hand* (great weather for MEDIA; Eds. Jane Ormerod, Thomas Fucaloro, Russ Green, David Lawton, George Wallace, and Mary McLaughlin Slechta)

JOHN AMEN is the author of three previous collections of poetry: *Christening the Dancer, More of Me Disappears,* and *At the Threshold of Alchemy.* He is co-writer, along with Daniel Y. Harris, of *The New Arcana,* a multi-genre work. In addition, he has released two folk/folk rock CDs: *All I'll Never Need* and *Ridiculous Empire.* He founded and continues to edit *The Pedestal Magazine.*

www.ingramcontent.com/pod-product-compliance
Lightning Source LLC
LaVergne TN
LVHW091226080426
835509LV00009B/1183